Cover illustration: Elements of the French 2nd Armoured Division move on to the Normandy beaches on 1 August. They were the first French-crewed tanks to return to France. The 2nd was held in reserve for the final drive to Paris for various reasons, not the least being the need to give the future French President, Charles De Gaulle, the honour of leading a French Division in the liberation of the French capital.

1. A column of M4s and an M10 tank destroyer enter the town of St. Lô on 20 July, thus setting the stage for Operation 'Cobra', the third and final attempt to break out from the Cotentin peninsula.

TANKS ILLUSTRATED NO.10

D-DAY
Tank Battles

BEACHHEAD TO BREAKOUT
GEORGE BALIN

a&ap

ARMS AND ARMOUR PRESS
London – Melbourne – Harrisburg, Pa. – Cape Town

Introduction

Tanks Illustrated 10: D-Day Tank Battles
Published in 1984 by
Arms and Armour Press, Lionel Leventhal
Limited, 2–6 Hampstead High Street, London
NW3 1QQ; 4–12 Tattersalls Lane, Melbourne,
Victoria 3000, Australia; Sanso Centre, 8 Adderley
Street, P.O. Box 94, Cape Town 8000; Cameron
and Kelker Streets, P.O. Box 1831, Harrisburg,
Pennsylvania 17105, USA

British Library Cataloguing in Publication Data
Balin, George
D-Day Tank Battles. – (Tanks illustrated; 10)
1. World War, 1939–1945 – Campaigns – France –
Normandy – Pictorial works 2. World War, 1939–
1945 – Tank warfare – Pictorial works
I. Title   II. Series
940.54´21´0222   D756.5.N6
ISBN 0-85368-633-5

Edited by Michael Boxall.
Layout by Roger Chesneau.
Printed and bound in Great Britain by William
Clowes Limited, Beccles and London.

*This book is dedicated to my mother Regina,
for her many years of support and
encouragement*

2. A Canadian Otter Mk I armoured car from an
unidentified reconnaissance regiment enters a
French town on the road to Le Mans in July 1944.
(Public Archives of Canada)

This June brings us the fortieth anniversary of Operation
'Overlord', the Allied invasion of the French mainland. It
began in the early hours of 6 June, 1944 with the dropping of
large numbers of American and British airborne forces.
These paratroopers were to be joined in the fighting later that
morning by thousands of American, British, Canadian,
French and Polish troops as the beach landings took place. To
say that the infantry bore the brunt of the fighting in
Normandy would be misleading; it is true that the infantry
had to fight their way inland from the beaches, but it was the
tank which led the way during the breakout in July/August.

The aim of this book is to give the reader a photographic
record of the various armoured vehicles which took part in
the fighting in the Normandy area from the landings in June,
throughout the breakout in July and August, to the liberation
of Paris in late August. Not surprisingly there are some areas
where photographic coverage is lacking; this is particularly
true with regard to photographs taken in the field by German
combat photographers. While there are a few pictures
available of German Tiger and Panther tanks in action, the
majority of these have been published many times.

Not every German armoured vehicle in Normandy was a
Tiger or a Panther. A great number were self-propelled
artillery vehicles or Panzerjägers. Furthermore, the Germans
made extensive use of vehicles that were local modifications
of French equipment captured in 1940. I have purposely
included coverage of these vehicles.

Unless otherwise stated, the majority of the photographs
have been selected from the US Army Signal Corps' files,
which form the Second World War Still Photographs section
in the US National Archives, and the Defense Audio-Visual
Agency, Washington, D.C. While coverage of the American
side of the fighting is very extensive, the same cannot be said
for the British involvement. This is because not all the tank
fighting took place near Caen, or in the 'Corridor of Death'
near the Falaise pocket. I have deliberately left the fighting in
the Falaise pocket out of this record because it has been
covered in numerous books and magazine articles. There was
just as much fighting further south in the Cherbourg
Peninsula, and it was there that the final breakout took place
in July.

I would like to express my sincere thanks to several friends
here in the States who kindly offered their assistance in the
preparation of this photographic record: Steve Zaloga,
probably the foremost authority in the USA on armoured
vehicles; Bill Auerbach, a specialist on late-war German
armoured vehicles, who furnished much information on
German equipment; the staff of the US National Archives,
particularly Mr. Paul White; and finally the staff of the
Defense Audio-Visual Agency, especially Ms. Regina
Strothers, who has offered her help time and time again over
many years. Without the gracious help of all these people,
this book would not have been possible.

George J. Balin, 1984

▲3 ▼4

3. Crewmen of a US Army M-16 anti-aircraft halftrack practise loading and off-loading from an LST somewhere in England. The constant practice helped to pass the time, easing the boredom caused by the postponements of the invasion because of adverse weather in the Channel.

4. The crew of an American M7 Priest named 'Big Chief III' prepare to board an LST at an unknown location on the south coast of England.

5. 'Hurricane', an M4 Sherman, moves ashore on Utah Beach on D Day. This was one of the first US tanks to land in France, and still has its wading gear attached.

6. A disabled M4 lies in a water filled shell-hole on one of the American beaches, most likely Utah. Of the many tanks lost near the beach-head, most fell victim to deep water or holes rather than to enemy action. Most crews were helpless in such cases and drowned.

7. A self-propelled 10.5cm leFH18(Sf) auf Geschützwagen 39H(f), probably of Panzer Battalion 100, moves up towards the front during the early hours of the invasion. In 1942, a total of 48 of these vehicles were converted, but none saw service outside France.

8. The vehicle illustrated represents a German modification on the French Hotchkiss H-39 to a self-propelled anti-tank gun. In German service, the type was designated the 10.5cm leFH18(Sf) auf Geschützwagen 39H(f); another variant was the 7.5cm PaK40(Sf) auf Geschützwagen 39H(f). A total of 72 vehicles were produced, and all of these were issued to Panzerartillerie and Panzerjäger units in France.

▼7

▼8

9. A destroyed 7.5cm PaK40/1 auf Geschützwagen Lorraine Schlepper (f) of which 170 were converted in 1942; of these, nearly 131 were still operational at the time of the invasion. Poorly armoured, they were no match for Allied tanks, or roaming ground attack aircraft.

10. An American Intelligence officer stands beside a captured German-modified Renault AMR35 tracked reconnaissance vehicle. More than a hundred of the little AMRs were captured in 1940, and many were converted to self-propelled carriers for the 8cm mortar. In German service the type was designated the 8cm schwerer Granatwerfer 34 auf Panzerspähwagen AMR35(f).

9 ▼

10 ▼

11. 'Virgin', an M4A4 Sherman of the 8th Tank Brigade moves ashore in Normandy, June 1944.

12. An M10 tank destroyer guards the approaches to the beaches a few days after the invasion. In the initial stages of the invasion the threat of German counterattacks was ever-present. The commander of this vehicle cautiously scans the sky for signs of enemy aircraft. Except for a short raid by a pair of FW-190 aircraft led by Oberstleutnant 'Pips' Priller of the Luftwaffe, little enemy aircraft activity presented itself.

▲ 13

13. A vintage, First World War, Renault FT17 light tank being examined by US infantrymen. In German service, the type was known as the Panzerkampfwagen FT-17 730(f). Huge quantities of these vehicles were captured by the Germans in 1940, and were put to use as security and anti-partisan vehicles.

14. A British Sherman Beach Armoured Recovery Vehicle (BARV) tows a truck on to the beaches in Normandy, June 1944. The BARV recovered vehicles that had been disabled, or submerged in deep water.

▼ 14

15▲ 16▼

15. A Humber Mk III armoured car of a British unit attached to the 21st Army Group guards the approaches to the landing beaches as infantrymen pass by on their way to the front lines. As the armoured car still carries its LST number, it is probable that this photograph was taken during the first few days of the invasion.

16. Elements of a British armoured car regiment move inland from the beaches during the early days of the invasion. They are passing a knocked-out Panzerkampfwagen IV which fell victim to either the intense naval bombardment, or the ever-present Allied fighter cover.

13

▲17 ▼18

19 ▲

17. A Ram OP tank moves inland during the early stages of the invasion. The Ram OP was the only turreted variant of the Ram series to see combat during the war. This particular vehicle no doubt belonged to an artillery regiment of the 3rd Canadian Division which landed at Juno Beach.

18. A British halftrack, with a 17pdr anti-tank gun in tow, negotiates a sharp bend in a French town during the early days of the invasion.

19. A British Sherman M4A4 moves through a town, cheered on by the locals. This photograph is believed to have been taken on D Day plus two in the town of La Déliverande on the road to Caen.

▲ 20

▲ 21

20. A British M4A1 Sherman negotiates a tight spot in a French street during the early days of the invasion.

21. An M4 'Crab' Mk I flail tank of the 1st Canadian Division moves inland with a column of armoured vehicles during the early stages of the invasion. The Canadians landed on Juno, and although delayed by strong tides and beach obstacles, managed to break out from the beach-head and move inland by nightfall.

22. 'Red Star', a Sherman 'Crab' flail tank of the 1st Lothians and Border Horse Armoured Regiment moves through a French city. A somewhat over-zealous censor obliterated the flail device from the photograph, but left the vehicle's markings intact.

23. A smoking 7.5cm Sturmgeschütz 40 ausf F tank destroyer lies beside the road on D Day plus four, probably a victim of a roving bazooka team clearing the way for troops on the move inland from the beaches.

24. This knocked-out Sd Kfz 250/9 bears mute testimony to the hazards of solo reconnaissance. These semi-tracked armoured cars when acting alone proved easy marks for infantry bazookas. This vehicle was blown apart by at least two separate penetrations.

▲25 ▼26

27 ▲

25. An M4 Sherman tank of the 2nd Armored Division rolls ashore on Omah Beach on D Day plus five; on this day, elements of the HQ unit and Combat Commands prepared the way for the rest of the division that was to follow.

26. An American halftrack, towing a 57mm anti-tank gun, passes a group of newly liberated French civilians on its way inland on 21 June.

27. Infantry from an unidentified unit cautiously look over a 4.7cm PaK(t) auf Panzerkampfwagen 35R(f) ohne Turm at an unknown location in France on 20 June 1944. A total of 174 of these vehicles were converted in 1941, and nearly 110 of them were still in service in France in 1944.

28. Members of an unidentified British armoured car regiment await orders to move out. The vehicle is the Canadian-produced Otter Mk I. The type served in Canadian and British units throughout the campaign in northwest Europe.

28 ▼

▲ 29   ▼ 30

31 ▲

29. Recently liberated French citizens make their way towards the Allied lines on 21 June 1944. They are passing a knocked out 7.5cm PaK40/1 auf Geschützwagen Lorraine Schlepper (f), of which 170 were converted for service in France. At the time of the invasion, nearly 131 were still operational.

30. Infantrymen of the 9th US Infantry Division, with a group of newly liberated French civilians, ride down a street in Cherbourg on 28 June. The vehicle is an Infanterie Schlepper UE 630(f), of French origin. Thousands of these vehicles were captured by the Germans in 1940, and many conversions were based on the chassis; these included a Panzerjäger version mounting the 3.7cm anti-tank gun, and a version mounting four Wurfrahmen 40.

31. Lying in a French wheatfield, a victim of offshore shelling, this Sturmpanzer IV Brummbär awaits recovery by a roaming tank recovery team. One of countless destroyed German armoured vehicles, it will be looked over, evaluated and then sent to the scrap-heap.

32. Before being destroyed, this Sd Kfz 250/9 leichter Schützenpanzerwagen (2cm) served with the 116th Panzer Division. This particular vehicle was based on the later 'Neu' variant of the Sd Kfz 250 armoured personnel carrier, and mounted the Hängelafette (swinging) 2cm turret; earlier versions mounted the complete turret from the Sd Kfz 222 leichter Panzerspähwagen (2cm).

32 ▼

▲33 ▼34

33. An American M7 Priest enters the liberated town of Carentan on 28 June. The drive into the Cherbourg area was complete.

34. 'Apache', an M4 with dozer blade, rolls down a road in Normandy. During the battles in the hedgerows, dozer tanks were used to plough through the 'bocage' to make way for the tanks following. At a later date an American sergeant named Cullin invented the 'Cullin' device, a structure welded to the nose of the tank to enable it to break through barriers.

35. Only 101 schwerer Panzerspähwagen (5cm) Sd Kfz 234/2 Puma armoured cars were built during the war. A total of 25 vehicles were attached to each Panzer-spähwagen Company of an armoured division. The vehicle illustrated probably belonged to the 2nd Panzer Division, a unit known to have operated the type in the Normandy area at the time of the invasion.

36. A damaged Sd Kfz 234/3 support armoured car lies beside the road in Normandy, June 1944. Barely visible on the nose is the leaping greyhound insignia of the 116th Panzer Division. This vehicle must have been one of the first examples of the type to enter service (production began in June 1944) and may well be the one which is now in the collection at Bovington in England.

37. This Möbelwagen 3.7cm FlaK proved no match for Allied ground attack aircraft. A total of 240 of the vehicles were produced and issued to the Flugabwehrzug (AA platoons) of Panzer regiments. They were very lightly armoured, and therefore very susceptible to air attack.

35 ▲

36 ▲

37 ▶

▲ 38

▲ 39

◀ 40

38. A group of vehicles lies in a field, probably victims of an Allied air attack. In the foreground is an anti-aircraft vehicle based on the Panzer 38(t), designated Flakpanzer 38(t) auf Selbst-fahrlafette 38(t). Only 140 were produced. The vehicle illustrated probably belonged to the 12th SS 'Hitler-jugend' Panzer Division.

39. A Morris scout car Mk II of an unidentified Canadian reconnais-sance regiment moves into Duberville on 9 July. (Public Archives of Canada

40. Two American infantrymen examine a Panzerkampfwagen V Panther ausf A, one of the many that were knocked out or abandoned during the battles of July and August.

41. A Nebelwerfer-armed Maultier lies abandoned in the Normandy 'bocage'. The Nebelwerfer left a conspicuous smoke trail which made it necessary for the vehicle to change its position after firing a salvo. The dense foliage of the 'bocage' was ideal for these weapons. This particular vehicle was probably disabled during the breakout in July.

42. An American infantryman peers into the fighting compartment of a knocked-out Wespe self-propelled gun. The Wespe was issued to SP detachments of Panzerartillerie regiments in Panzer and Panzergrenadier divisions from 1943 onwards. The vehicle was very small and easily concealed; it would emerge, fire a few rounds and return to its hiding-place.

43. An American sergeant looks over a knocked-out Panzerjäger 38(t) mit 7.5cm PaK40/3 ausf M (Marder III) in a Normandy hedgerow. This vehicle was destroyed in early July, probably by an Allied aircraft.

44. An M5A1 Stuart of the 3rd Armored Division, held up in the congestion at the stone bridge at Airel. After heavy fighting, elements of Combat Command B managed to get across the bridge on 8 July. Without artillery support, the various units engaged began to move southwest across the River Vire into an area dominated by roads and hedgerows; the months of hedgerow fighting were to begin in earnest.

45. An M4A1 Sherman attached to the US 30th Infantry Division moves past a pair of knocked-out Panzerkampfwagen IV ausf Js. The Panzer IVs served with the 2nd SS Panzer Division 'Das Reich', and were knocked out along the bridgehead between St. Fromond and St. Lô on 9 July 1944.

46. American infantryman Private Ward Watley of Texas, peers into one of a pair of knocked-out Panzerkampfwagen V Panther ausf As knocked-out in the Normandy 'bocage' during the second week of July. The rope running from the muzzle brake of the vehicle was an attempt to warn unwary Allied troops of the possibility of booby-traps.

◄43

▼44

45 ▲　46 ▼

▲47 ▼48

47. A pair of Panzerkampf-wagen Panther ausf A tanks knocked out on a road near Le Désert on 11 July 1944. These tanks belonged to the Panzer Lehr Division, and were two of more than fifty armoured vehicles that the Division lost to air and land attack on that day. The abortive counter-attack by Panzer Lehr cost the division more than a quarter of its strength.

48. An American M10 attached to the 30th US Infantry Division moves into a position in the Normandy 'bocage' near St. Jean-de-Daye on 11 July. Fighting had raged all week along the Airel–St. Jean-de-Daye road as elements of the 30th Infantry Division and 3rd Armored Division made for the stone bridge across the River Vire at Airel.

49. An impromptu repair shop is set up in the town square of St. Jean-de-Daye on 11 July. A pair of the newly-issued M4A1 (76mm) Sherman tanks are evident; one already having a pile of sandbags on the hull front to increase the armoured protection.

52 ▲

50. An M5A1 Stuart of the 3rd Armored Division makes its way into the town of St. Fromond on 11 July.

51. M4s armed with 105mm howitzers firing from a French wheatfield on 13 July 1944. They are probably providing fire support for units attempting to break out of the hedgerows at Hill 122 near Carillon during the drive on St. Lô.

52. An M5A1 Stuart turns a corner in the town of St. Paul de Verney on 17 July. This vehicle, nicknamed 'Concrete', was a standard production M5A1 with the exposed M20 machine-gun mount.

▲ 53　▼ 54

53. 'Corregidor', an M12 self-propelled 155mm gun fires in support of forces in action near St. Lô on 16 July. The M12 was extremely effective during the breakout and quite often provided the only heavy support available.

54. A British M7 Priest provides fire support during the battles of July.

55. An M7 Priest of an unidentified British artillery regiment fires in support during the early stages of Operation 'Goodwood' on 18 July.

56. Carriers of an unidentified motor battalion race through a town on the way to the front during the bitter fighting of July. Casualties among the crews were high because of the lack of any overhead protection which left them exposed to shells bursting above.

▲ 57

▲ 58

57. A British M4A4 Sherman races to the front during the opening stages of Operation 'Goodwood' on 18 July. This operation was to set the stage for the British drive on Caen. During the operation the British 11th Armoured Division was very badly mauled, losing 126 tanks, or more than half its strength.

58. British Sherman tanks from an unidentified armoured brigade pass a knocked-out Sd Kfz 222 armoured car. It is unusual to see this vehicle so late in the war as more modern types such as the Sd Kfz 234 Puma became available; obviously at a crucial time everything was pressed into service.

59. A British Daimler Mk II armoured car brings up the rear. While a censor has removed the unit markings, the roof identification star is still visible. It is probable that this vehicle belonged to the 2nd Derbyshire Yeomanry Regiment, the reconnaissance regiment of the 51st (Highland) Division, one of the follow-up divisions landed in Normandy. The photograph was taken somewhere near Caen during the fighting in the Scottish Corridor in late July.

60. A British tank column enters Ecouché, led by an M4A4 Sherman and followed up by a Loyd Carrier with a 6pdr anti-tank gun in tow.

61. An M5A1 Stuart makes its way cautiously into the town of St. Lô on 20 July 1944. The liberation of the town was achieved after the Americans' second attempt to break out of the Cotentin peninsula. The operation began on 13 July and ended five days later with the liberation of St. Lô; but only at the cost of nearly 11,000 casualties. American tankers learned quickly about the danger of the 'Panzerfaust', and devised ways to protect themselves. This vehicle has piles of sandbags to boost its protection.

62. An American M10 of an unidentified tank destroyer battalion lies among the rubble of St. Lô. The dead crew lie near the relatively undamaged vehicle, mute testimony to the danger of tanks outrunning their infantry support. During the early stages of the taking of the town, there were many instances when both sides overran their own positions. The crew of this vehicle were caught in the open.

61▶

▼62

63 ▲

63. A knocked-out Panther ausf A and an Sd Kfz 251/7 ausf D mittlerer Pionierpanzerwagen (engineer vehicle) lie on the road from St. Lô to Périers. On the morning of 24 July elements of the Panzer Lehr reported that the Americans had begun to vacate positions west of St. Lô for no apparent reason. They would soon realize that Operation 'Cobra', the third and final attempt to break out from the Cotentin peninsula had begun; for on the morning of the 25th, waves of B-17s began their bombing runs.

64. This 15cm Panzerwerfer 42 auf Sf (Sd Kfz 4/1), known as the Maultier, lies on the road from St. Lô. The vehicle was no doubt knocked-out during the massive bombing and shelling which accompanied the breakout from St. Lô during Operation 'Cobra'. The Maultier was the standard vehicle of the self-propelled Nebelwerfer brigades, and was produced in both an armed variant (as illustrated) and as an ammunition carrier (Munitionskraftwagen für Nebelwerfer, Sd Kfz 4).

64 ▼

65. Infantrymen from one of the three US Infantry Divisions which led the advance during 'Cobra', pass a disabled Panther ausf A of the Panzer Lehr Division. This division was caught in the massive bombings which preceded 'Cobra' and was virtually destroyed. By that time the US 4th, 9th and 30th Infantry Divisions had begun their drive along the St. Lô–Périers road. Initially slowed down by massive craters, the breakthrough was under way within a few days.

▲ 66

66. Infantrymen pass an M4A1 Sherman of 'D' Coy of either the 66th or 67th Armored Regiment of the US 2nd Armored Division, during the drive out of the Cotentin peninsula towards Coutances, late July 1944.

67. Elements of the US 2nd Armored Division pass a pair of knocked-out Panzerkampfwagen IV ausf H tanks during the drive out from the Cotentin peninsula towards Coutances in late July 1944.

68. A US M10 tank destroyer passes a First World War memorial in an unidentified French town during the late stages of the breakout in July.

67 ▼

▼ 68

69. An M31B1 recovery tank makes its way down a road near St. Cilles on 26 July. The M31 was used to recover damaged or captured tanks and was based on the old M3 Lee/Grant series. It was the only version of the M3 to see service in the northwest Europe campaign.

70. An M7 Priest moves through a small forest during the latter stages of the breakout on 29 July. The vehicle is shown passing a memorial to several German soldiers killed during the earlier battles of June.

71

▲72

71. Infantrymen examine a Sturmgeschütz IV (7.5cm StuK40 L/48) for booby-traps at an unknown location on 29 July 1944. Considering that more than 1,100 of these vehicles were produced, it is surprising that very few photographs of the vehicle in service have appeared.

72. An M4A3 Sherman passes a US 57mm anti-tank gun in Mont Brocard on 29 July. In the background lies an abandoned Sd Kfz 251 ausf D armoured personnel carrier. It is unusual to see the limited-issue camouflage uniforms because by this time they had been ordered to be withdrawn from service; similarity to Waffen SS patterns had led to a number of fatal incidents.

73. Elements of the heavy self-propelled artillery battalion of the 2nd SS Panzer Division 'Das Reich' lie destroyed on a road near St. Denis-de-Gastines. On 29 July they had run into the bivouac of the US 78th Armored Field Artillery Battalion whose 3in guns decimated the column of eleven vehicles. The vehicles are unusual in that they still carry divisional insignia so late into the campaign. In addition, the 15cm Hummel bears a personal name on its side.

74. An M4 (105mm-armed) Sherman moves down a road in Coutances on 29 July. The howitzer-armed tanks often led the pack because of their better armoured mantlet and heavier gun. Until the introduction of the M4A3E2 'Jumbo' tanks, with their massive additional armour on the hull front, later in the campaign in northwest Europe, the M4 (105mm) had to perform the task of point duty.

75. A 3rd Armored Division M4A3 makes its way down a street in Coutances on 31 July. To its right lies a knocked-out M5A1, a victim of the random mines left by the retreating German forces on the 29th.

◀73

76. A well-camouflaged M5A1 Stuart makes its way through Coutances on 30 July. Barely visible on the hull front is the standard yellow bridging circle. This device showed the vehicle's weight in tons and helped to avoid accidents on make-shift bridges.

77. Elements of the US 3rd Armored Division make their way into Coutances on 31 July 1944. Most of the town had been destroyed by massive Allied artillery and aerial bombardment. A hard day-long battle had ensued between forces of the US 3rd Armored Division and the German 2nd and 17th SS Panzer Divisions, who had fought a brave rearguard action. The Germans were eventually forced to pull out when elements of the US 4th and 6th Armored Divisions appeared.

78. A column of M4s await the order to move out from Coutances on 31 July 1944. The lead tank mounts a 75mm gun, the second has a 105mm howitzer. Lessons hard learned in the hedgerows taught tankers that the conspicuous white stars had to be painted out because they provided an aiming-point for anti-tank gunners. These tanks are most likely of the US 3rd Armored Division.

▲76

▲77 ▼78

79. American tankers watch as members of the French Resistance march a collaborator past their M4A3 Sherman. The French population went to great lengths to punish those who had sided with the Germans during the occupation. The lucky ones were publicly humiliated, and had their heads shaved.

80. Three M4A3 (75mm) Shermans lie smoking in a field a few miles outside Avranches. They belonged to the US 4th Armored Division, and were knocked out during the division's drive for the bridges over the River See by 88mm anti-tank guns emplaced along the bluffs which dominate the bridges. This was only a minor setback, as tanks from the 4th managed to roll across the unguarded Pontaubault Bridge on 31 July. This allowed the Americans to break out of the Cotentin peninsula, the last natural defence line before Brittany.

81. Elements of an unidentified tank battalion move through a field during the August breakout. This M4A3 loaded with infantrymen passes a knocked-out late-production Sd Kfz 11 3-ton armoured personnel carrier.

79▲

80▲ 81▼

N.176
AVRANCHES
MANCHE

▲82

▲83   ▼84

82. The breakout fully underway, a pair of M5 Stuarts move down the road leading to Avranches on 31 July. Elements of the US 4th Armored Division were able to cross an unguarded bridge over the River See, and make their way into Brittany. Lying across the back deck of the vehicles is the cerise air identification panel issued to tanks to prevent strafing by Allied fighters.

83. An M4 of the 8th Tank Battalion, 4th Armored Division, rolls through a tank obstacle near Avranches on 31 July 1944. The 8th Tank Battalion was one of the most camouflage-conscious units in the 4th Armored Division, having gone to great lengths to paint out the conspicuous white ID stars, etc. In addition, they were one of the few units that repainted their vehicles in random camouflage patterns, perhaps with mud; they also welded fittings to allow foliage to be attached.

84. Members of the US 3rd Armored Division examine a knocked-out 7.5cm Sturmgeschütz 40 ausf F/8 which was destroyed during the post-Operation 'Cobra' advances near Roncey on 1 August 1944.

85. An American M4 moves through the rubble-filled streets of Roncey on 1 August. This vehicle is unusual in that it still carries the conspicuous white ID stars on its nose, and hull sides. Quite often photographs of knocked-out Allied tanks show one or two neat penetrations directly through the hull side stars. Most crews resorted to painting them out with either black or olive drab paint.

86. Elements of an armoured infantry regiment's rifle company passing through Roncey on 1 August. The few remaining townspeople watch as an American halftrack passes by towing a 37mm anti-tank gun. In the background a knocked-out Sd Kfz 7 Flakvierling can be seen among the rubble.

85▲   86▼

▲87

▲88   ▼89

48

87. During a lull in the fighting, a lone French woman walks amidst the havoc of war in Roncey. The pair of Panzerjäger 38(t) mit 7.5cm PaK40/3 ausf M (Marder IIIs) were but two of the many German AFVs destroyed in the area during the fighting on 1 August.

88. 'Tarentaise', an M4A2 of the French 2nd Armoured Division, makes its way on to the Normandy beaches on 1 August. The Sherman was the mainstay of the division, with three regiments using the type. The M3A3 Stuart was used by the reconnaissance regiment, while the M10 was used by the tank-destroyer regiment.

89. American troops enter Torigni-sur-Vire on 3 August 1944. Only three days before, a mistake by the German troops occupying the surrounding area allowed elements of the British 11th Armoured Division to pour through the Forêt l'Eveque, thus leaving the south bank of the River Souloeuvre and the high ground east of the River Vire open for US infantry to advance.

90. An American reconnaissance jeep moves to the rear with a captured German sniper, passing a column of M4 Shermans which are making their way into Brittany on 3 August. The sniper proved a great threat to the exposed tank commanders, who were easy marks. This fellow should consider himself lucky not to have been taken behind a tree and shot.

91. A newly-issued M4A1 (76mm) Sherman of the 67th Armored Regiment, 2nd Armored Division, enters St. Sever-Calvados on 3 August. It took the unit nearly five days to enter the town because the Germans had destroyed the only bridge and commanded the heights above the approaches to it. In the course of the action, the 67th lost a number of tanks to concealed anti-tank guns.

92. An M5A1 Stuart and M10 tank destroyer attached to the 66th Armored Regiment of the US 2nd Armored Division cover the approaches to Tessy-sur-Vire. The town had fallen on 2 August when the 66th's 2nd Battalion in support of the US 120th Infantry Regiment, 30th Infantry Division managed to enter after several days of hard fighting. The infantry had been pinned down for more than a day, but when four M4A3s managed to get into the town the defending troops fled.

90 ▲

91 ▲ 92 ▼

▲ 93

93. This disabled Wespe, its howitzer locked in death, was found abandoned in August in the Normandy 'bocage'. The type served with the self-propelled detachments of Panzerartillerie regiments in both Panzer and Panzergrenadier divisions from 1943 onwards. In service it was designated leichte Feldhaubitze 18/2 auf Fahrgestell Panzerkampfwagen II (Sf) (Sd Kfz 124).

94. Tanks of the 66th or 67th Armored Regiment, 2nd Armored Division, advance through hedgerows outside Champ-du-Bouet on 10 August. The leading tank is one of the rare M4A1 (76mm) Shermans that got into the Normandy fighting. At the time of the invasion, nearly 300 of them were available, but many commanders were hesitant to replace their 75mm-armed tanks as it was unproven in combat. Once the units encountered the Tiger and Panther, it became obvious that a larger gun was needed.

95. 'Laxative', an American M8 HMC, prepares to fire in support of an infantry attack, near Barénton on 9 August. A 'Cullin' hedgerow device is attached to its nose. Before firing it was necessary to check that the barrel was clear of the large amounts of foliage used for camouflage.

96. Elements of the 1st Infantry Division, 'Big Red One', make their way past a knocked-out M4 of the 3rd Armored Division in Mortain on 3 August. This vehicle was knocked out by a Panzerfaust during a spearhead attack by the division into the town. The American troops expected to conduct a mopping-up operation, but were forced out during fierce German counter-attacks later that day. The Germans held the town until overwhelming American forces drove them out for good on 7 August.

▼ 94

◄97

97. US infantry pass a knocked-out Panzerkampfwagen IV ausf H of the 2nd Panzer Division in Pont-Farcy on 3 August.
98. M8 armoured cars of the 2nd Armored Division's reconnaissance company make their way through St. Sever-Calvados on 3 August.

98 ▲

99. A 'deuce-and-a-half' truck passes a knocked-out Panzerkampfwagen IV ausf H of the 2nd Panzer Division. The divisional trident insignia is barely visible near the driver's vision device. This vehicle was put out of action during the first week of August.

99 ▼

102 ▲

103 ▲

104 ▲ 105 ▼

100. M4s of the 3rd Armored Division make their way through a gully near Reffuveille on 7 August. The attacks which followed eventually led to the re-taking of the town of Mortain which had been lost to German counterattacks earlier that week.

101. This Sd Kfz 250 armoured personnel carrier was part of an entire company of armoured vehicles of the 2nd Panzer Division which were knocked out on 14 August near St. Aubin d'Appenai. They had the misfortune to run into a trap set by a US tank-destroyer battalion attached to the 30th Infantry Division.

102. Disabled late-production Sd Kfz 250 'Neu' models lie beside the road in an unidentified French town in August 1944.

103. GIs from an unidentified infantry unit advance past a disabled Unic Kegresse P107 armoured personnel carrier during the latter stages of the August fighting. In German service the vehicle was designated as the leichter Schützenpanzerwagen U304(f) and appeared in a number of different variants, being used mainly as lightly armoured personnel carriers, ambulances and artillery tractors.

104. A knocked-out 15cm sFH13/1 (Sf) auf Geschützwagen Lorraine Schlepper (f) lies in a French field, destroyed during one of the many battles in August. A total of 94 of these vehicles were converted in 1942 for service in the various Panzerartillerie Abteilungs. At the time of the invasion 54 were still available, the rest having been lost during the campaign in North Africa.

105. A knocked-out late-production 7.5cm Sturmgeschütz 40 ausf G lies abandoned in a hayfield somewhere in France in late August. These vehicles proved very effective in bocage country because of their low silhouette. Unwary Allied tanks made easy targets.

106. Members of an American Intelligence team examine captured German armoured vehicles in a tank park at the end of the September fighting. A large amount of German equipment was captured, including many vehicles of French origin. Vehicles seen here include Panzerkampfwagen 38H and 39H 735(f), a Munitionsschlepper 35R 731(f), and a Marder III 7.5cm PaK40/3 auf Panzerkampfwagen 38(t) ausf H (Sd Kfz 138).

107. An American M7 prepares to fire in support of a nearby infantry attack near Anet on 20 August. The M7 HMC and the M8 HMC were the backbone of the American self-propelled artillery force throughout the war.

▲106 ▼107

108. The large amounts of German equipment captured during the battles of August and September were gathered into depots to be examined by Allied Intelligence teams. Many of the vehicles eventually made their way into museums. Unfortunately, many of the more unusual vehicles disappeared for ever. The vehicle seen here is an armoured reconnaissance vehicle based on the Panzer 38(t). In service it was designated Aufklärer auf Fahrgestell Panzerkampfwagen 38(t) mit 2cm KwK38. Very few were produced, probably only about fifty in all. This one is believed to have served in either the 2nd or 116th Panzer Division in the Normandy area.

109. A Humberette Mk I scout car of a Canadian regiment awaiting orders to move out from a French town in late August 1944. (Public Archives of Canada)

▲111

110. (Previous spread) A Morris Scout Car Mk II leads a column of armoured cars of the RAF Regiment into the town of Pont-Royal on 23 August. The RAF Regiment used a number of different types of armoured car including the Morris Scout Car and Humber armoured car. In addition, a number of M4 Shermans were used as OP tanks to guide Allied air strikes.

111. A French policeman watches crew members of the American halftrack, 'Excitement', reload the pedestal-mounted 50cal machine-gun; August 1944

112. Cheering French citizens wave on an American halftrack as it passes through an unidentified town late in August. The massive amounts of personal gear carried by these vehicles is evident here.

▼112

113. Elements of the French 2nd Armoured Division (2e Division Blindée) await orders to begin the final drive to liberate Paris. After four long years of occupation the heart of France was to be free once more. By 23 August the division was more than 120 miles away; however, they soon began a mad dash down the departmental roads to Paris, and by the 25th the city was free. There were three regiments in the division operating the M4A2: the 501e Régiment de Chars de Combat, the 12e Régiment de Chasseurs d'Afrique, and the 12e Régiment de Cuirassiers.

114. On 23 August tanks of the French 2nd Armoured Division wait for the order to move out for Paris. The M4A2 and M3A3 were the two main tanks used by the division. All French tanks carried personal names; those of the Chars de Combat bore the names of past French battles of the Napoleonic Wars and the First World War. The tanks of the Cuirassiers used names of the first French towns to be liberated during the invasion; the Chasseurs preferred the names of past Marshals from the Imperial period, or names of the old royal provinces. The M10s of the Fusiliers-Marins, the divisional tank-destroyer unit, used the names of the various maritime trade winds.

117▲

115. An American M4A3 Sherman enters a French town on the outskirts of Paris on 25 August. American troops were held back in order to allow elements of the French 2nd Armoured Division the honour of liberating the French capital.

116. M3A3 Stuart tanks of the French 2nd Armoured Division (2e Division Blindée) pass cheering crowds during the liberation of Paris on 25 August. The vehicles illustrated belong to the 1er Régiment de marche des Spahis marocains, a colonial unit which formed the reconnaissance regiment of the division.

117. After four years of occupation, groups of newly-liberated Parisians mill about abandoned German equipment in one of the city's many squares. Fighting had erupted in Paris on the morning of 19 August and cost members of the Resistance more than 125 killed. On 20 August a truce was arranged, but this fell apart on the 21st and fighting began anew. By Tuesday, 22 August the fighting began to turn the insurgents' way. Wednesday, 23 August emerged as the day that the French 2e Division Blindée began its final drive to liberate Paris.

118. Elements of the 2e Division Blindée move past the Lion of Belfort, a monument to the French resistance to the Prussians during the 1871 Franco-Prussian War. The column is led by halftracks of the Régiment de marche de Tchad, the divisional motor infantry regiment; following close behind are M4A2 Shermans of the 12e Régiment de Cuirassiers. The division had managed to cover more than 120 miles to reach Paris on 25 August and by the end of the day Paris once again was French.

118▼

▲119

119. Tanks of the 2e Division Blindée were not the only French-crewed tanks in Paris on the day of liberation. This Char de Bataille B1 bis operated by members of the Forces Françaises de l'Intérieur (FFI) was there to meet their countrymen as they entered the centre of the city on 25 August.

120. American M8 armoured cars from an armoured reconnaissance unit sweep past a crowd in the Champs-Elysées on 29 August. Paris was a free city. All that remained to be done was to arrange for aid to reach the population, and to gear up for the drive to the Siegfried Line and Germany itself.

▼120